A TWIST C

Also by Joy Howard

SECOND BITE
(with Hilary J Murray and Gina Shaw)

A TWIST OF MALICE

Uncomfortable Poems by Older Women

Edited by Joy Howard

GREY HEN

First published in 2008 by Grey Hen Press
PO Box 450
Keighley
West Yorkshire
BD22 9WS
www.greyhenpress.com

ISBN 978-0-9552952-2-5

Printed by:
Q3 Print Project Management Ltd
Loughborough
Leicestershire
LE11 1LE

Thanks are due to Barbara Burford for her ongoing support and encouragement; Gina Shaw for casting an eagle eye over the final manuscript; Anne Stewart for always being on hand with a helpful response; David Tipton for kindly sharing his publishing know-how, and every single one of the poets whose work you are about to enjoy for their enthusiasm and generosity throughout the process.

By the pricking of my thumbs,
Something wicked this way comes:

Shakespeare: *Macbeth*

Preface

First and foremost, this anthology is meant to entertain. It has certainly been a huge pleasure collecting the poems, communicating with the poets and editing the manuscript.

There are scary bits, and things that go bump in the night, and a more than average aura of menace, but also a deep vein of humour. That's good then – we may be cracking on a bit, and we all have some scars, but we're still smiling. You can't keep a good poet down – and there are plenty of very good poets proving the point in this anthology.

But while you won't, I hope, end up the sadder for reading this book, you may well end up the wiser. There's a wealth of life experience in here, related by women who, in spite of everything, haven't lost the life force. You can feel it come crackling off the page.

So I hope everyone that reads it finds plenty to smile about, but – keep your eyes skinned and don't turn your back....

Joy Howard

Contents

All's Well that Ends Badly

Ghosts, Ghouls & Visitations

Hellhags & Changelings

You Have Been Warned

Shape Shifting

And Another Thing ...

All's Well that Ends Badly

Bonfire Night

Let there be sparklers
and pumpkin lanterns
and Roman Candles and Catherine Wheels
on the night that I burn
the tatters of his wedding suit
on a fire in the garden.

Let there be rockets
and sidewinders, crackerjacks
and golden showers
and an almighty conflagration
on the night that I fan
the orange and outraged flames to consume
his lying letters of love.

Let there be toffee apples
and hot chocolate in flasks
and potatoes baked in the fire
to keep my hands warm
on the night I stir into the ashes
his uneaten dinners
his unslept-on sheets.

Let there be sparks
spiralling up on the breeze
and floating unnoticed
in through open windows
and smouldering in cheap furniture
turning to flames licking around
the edges of rooms, consuming
dirty carpets and old kitchen units
on the night I make an end
to unpainted doors and unfinished jobs.

Let there be pennies
for the guy
when the insurance company refuses
to pay for the damage
as he's under-insured –
not having any notion
he's had it coming for years.

Rosemary McLeish

Revenge Tragedy

There wasn't a real murder – or any blood
for that matter. But on my left wrist
there's still the faint pink ghost
of a carpet burn from the Somalian rug –
the one that's in your living room.

Those times when I took things lying down
haunt me like clichés in a bad romance.
I never got you back – that's the tragedy of it.

Kathryn Daszkiewicz

Misreading the Entrails

That time your bay horse went lame
and we sat in the barn
smoking Passing Clouds
and watching butterflies
swarm over the privet bush
and the poor horse resting
one pointed hoof on the ground
that way they do when it hurts them
and the shadows lengthening
in the late-afternoon hush
and I was just thinking
how I could stay there
with you almost for ever
and that you would kiss me
any time now
and it was about then
when you threw away your cigarette
and I yelled at you, because of the hay
and you said *OK, OK, I'm sorry* –
and told me that the next day
you were off to be a priest
and I laughed and punched you
because it was such a good joke –
only the way life turned out
things weren't all that funny
and so, though it's been great
to see you again
and no, the child isn't yours,
believe me, I would far rather
eat a load of your old horse's shit
than call you Father.

Angela Kirby

Ties

It mocks me *sotto voce* from the wardrobe;
out, it is a jazz of orange stripes.
You wore it once to kick
against convention, haven't put it on
for years. It was a present from the woman
we don't talk about.

I grip the scissors, slip the lower blade
inside the silky point and press until
my arm is fully stretched. Threads part,
warp and weft in one long sweep,
facings and linings lie revealed. The sound
is like a long-held sigh.

What next? The old school falls
in a blue-gold tangle; on top writhe
regimental snakes. Tired of the lisp of silk,
I reach for polyester, the company-logo'd red;
the sibilance is higher. Knitted wool needs snips
as deep as groans.

This is a serenade for scissors,
but what part for Harris tweed?
It's tough and growls as the right arm drops;
lapels show their teeth. Gaberdine
rasps from vent to nape, linen has crunch,
waxed cloth whines.

Now I need the purr of cashmere
with its smell of some elusive thing
I do not like. But it's Tuesday and the Club
straight from the office; you're wearing it
and won't be home till late.
Well, I can wait.

Gill Learner

Marriage

In our unspokeness lies
the acceptance which years
have proved

        our unspokeness lies

           Ruth O'Callaghan

Sisters

You pinched me in the pram
when I was too young to tell,
left bruises on my arm

but I bathed your Queenie doll
and rusted her voice box
so she couldn't say mama.

           Carole Bromley

Small Slam in Hearts

The woman sitting
with her back to me,
her perfect slender
and gathered back, the shoulders
straight and light,
the waist a mouth
for the vase of her hips,
the long water of her perfect calves,
is wearing a smoky rose
dress with big cream buttons
down the spine. Working buttons.
Meaning, it's the only way
she can climb in or out of her clothes.
One button for each knuckle. One button
for each segment of the worm, one
for each of her lover's finger pads
as he dials his cell phone.
"I think you're lying," he whispers
and wipes his lips on the cream
coloured mouthpiece. But she doesn't hear
the ringing. She's playing cards.

Jude Goodwin

Here's Another Poem

Here's another poem to lay at your feet.
Or to ram down your throat now that
you can't criticise my style, or do a
rewrite, or tell me poetry doesn't count,
never meant anything to you, didn't
come anywhere near science for clarity,
purity, importance, or meaning. Dear
Dad, now that I can get a word in edgeways,
as many as I want to, and more, as
you retreat further into the silence of non-
being, no longer the silence of the
shut study door, what will I say?

Here is another poem to lay at your feet,
another drawing, another bouquet of roses.

Rosemary McLeish

When You've Gone

I shall make myself an omelette
which I shall eat in bed,
and wash down
with a half-litre
of Rioja or,
on second thoughts,
a whole one, and
I shall lick the plate
and read all night
surrounded by
fluffy pink hot-water bottles
then fall asleep
with the radio
or my vibrator on
and, dearheart, believe me,
these are just some
of the many small but
not-inconsiderable joys
which console me in
your many absences
while above all, and
please take note,
this is now a wind-free zone.

Angela Kirby

The Nth Day of Christmas

My dear,
I wish you a Busby Berkeley hell
of strictly choreographed thighs;
metronome smiles, and crotches
in relentless three-four time.

Oh, may you drown in ostrich feathers.
OD on dimpled whimsy.
And all this before
fifty-two matched white pianos
fall on you.

Not entering into the spirit?
Losing my sense of frivolity?
Bitter, twisted and frustrated?
Damn Right!

Barbara Burford

Karma

She said *you're doing something very wrong*
and disapproval clouded up the day
soured the champagne, let the sun illuminate
my wrinkles so I really looked like hell
made me step in dogshit on the lawn
and put a dragon in my best friend's place.
I'd wanted her to give me some advice
and here she was white and withdrawn.

It had started with a Diva ad.
This woman lived in Liverpool and though
we'd only spoken briefly on the phone
both sitting on our separate flight of stairs
I think there was some kind of little death
though whose it was I must say I forget
I just remember one of us had groaned.
Her photos were impressive with that hat
she said there wasn't anybody else.
Of course she lied but how was I to know.

I came home from that party by myself
we didn't speak best part of a year.
Friends tried to get us to get over it
to no avail. I could not forgive
that word *wrong*, there was some kind of truce.
Then she said she'd got involved with someone
who had children and a wedding ring.
Overnight the dragon disappeared
my friend came back. Of course I didn't gloat
I never say a thing.

Berta Freistadt

A cold cafe, the three of us,

and the waiter asking *Are you the meat?*

No, I say. I am the plain vegetarian quiche,
bitter green salad with herbs, no dressing.
She is the Chateaubriand, *avec truffes.*
He is the well-hung game, marinaded in stout,
side order of chips.

      Who's for pudding? He asks.
No pudding for me, but she will have
Death by Chocolate, sprinkled with
hundreds and thousands.
He will have upside down pudding,
topped with full dairy cream.

      And to follow?
I will have coffee, strong, black, no sugar.
She will have latte, sponge fingers.
He will have Irish coffee,
brandy to follow.

They will be leaving early.
I will be picking up the bill.

                  Ann Alexander

Miss You Nights

I dreamt more that winter.
People trooped through cityscapes
in black and white and I couldn't say
whether they were from my past
or from the films I sat through
in an alcoholic half-haze after lunch.

And you never bothered to turn up,
though I lay curled like a comma
under the duvet punctuating
my own impatience, whimpering
in the dark, trying to conjure you
out of nothing. Typical.

I grew increasingly obsessive,
devised a summoning ritual
before sleep where I imagined
I took your upper lip between my lips
and crimped it gently like pie crust,
fluted it with my teeth. But it didn't work.

And the togs I slept under, duck down
and eider feather, shifted around
and fanned themselves into a froth,
going on and on about being pulled
out of warm skin, about puckered
sting-marks smarting like cold sores,

saying everything was my fault.
Which it obviously wasn't. Not you
or what happened to your family
afterwards. Considering I caused it
I think under the circumstances
I was entirely blameless.

Marianne Burton

14

The Cutters' Daughter

On the kitchen table
he cut out her scarlet jacket
marking it with tailor's chalk,
white for her, blue for me:
my eyes wandered the cool ribbons of colour.
Years later I found their photographs:
buying the ruby ring, and then
the two of them, young, untouched
on a bright July day before a Gothic arch.
My mother was beautiful, brunette,
a 1930s dream, white dress and veil:
her roses stream to the ground
their falling petals vivid confetti
against the ineffectual horseshoe.
My father, ash-blonde and dreamy-needy,
had a 'cat that got the cream' expression
on his face. Or so she said.
At that moment she was thinking,
'What have I done'? Even then as the camera clicked.

I notice the blunt effect of the scissors on the snap
where once she tried to cut him out.

Thelma Laycock

The White Garden

I'm going to rip out the iceberg roses,
the rocket whose sweetness,
after dark, attracts the moths,
the Madonna lilies and myrtle
and pale bleeding hearts;
inject the heat of marigolds
and blowsy orange poppies
and plant that rose as black
as a woman's blood before it flows.
I'll call a truce with aphids
and the choking fronds of creepers,
stop cutting back the nettles
and cleaning out the pond.
I'll let the sycamore saplings grow
until they're giants against the sun,
and leeches breed in damp places
among the leaves, and snakes thick
as a man's arm infest the trees.
There'll be no peace: the air
will be full of rustlings and cries.
And in the twilight of the underforest
I'll be there, waiting for you
with my pipe and poison darts.

Ruth Sharman

The Reunion

After three months he returned.
It's been too long, he moaned,
twisting in her arms. He sighed
over her cooking, called it sexy,
whispered that her secret blend
of garlic, chilli, lemon grass
and thyme had given the salmon
a sublimely dangerous edge,
that the bottle of *Gros Plant*
was flirty and, for once,
had travelled well
then made love to her again
so when, perhaps by accident,
he hit play-back
on his answering-machine
and when, between those
chummy messages from his dentist –
something about bridge-work –
and from his mother, three times,
and some breezy chums
suggesting golf, when then,
a younger voice breathed
Mon Amour, Je t'aime!
she reached out for the fish-knife
and slashed down
swift and sure.

Angela Kirby

17

Clean Break

After the strife and the cold *stuff you*
I vacuumed him out of my life
with my Dyson DC07, Mk II.

The Dyson's moans drowned out my own
as I watched his motes and beams fly round
the polycarbonate plastic drum.

I sucked the bugger in! I seized
the see-thru serpentine flexible hose,
sought him in every corner and crease.

And all the dirty things he said
were caught by the cyclone-action spin,
and filtered out. I wanted him dead –

Dust to dust. Smooth textured, fine.
I emptied him out on the compost heap,
with the half finished bottle of wine.

Ann Alexander

Cutting Edge

I like my poems better now
less imagery
sharper
more honest
and direct
like pain

But I will like them better still
when I can write
in more removed
and philosophical a style
love you dear and let you go
with a wry smile

Joy Howard

Ghosts, Ghouls & Visitations

There is No Moon

There is no moon and the air is damp.
Beyond the bushes bordering the park
something is brooding in the rancid dark.
I race with my shadow from lamp to lamp.

My ears catch something slinking in my wake.
It stops when I stop. A sly breeze
stirs the twigs which try to seize
my sleeve as I pass. My stretched eyes ache.

At home the lock's capricious. I fumble my key,
stumble, and trip into brooding dark.
Whatever it was that watched from the park
has sidled into the house with me.

Gina Shaw

Donna La Morte

A weighty flutter overhead.
An owl comes out of the night
moves through darkness to settle.
Donna La Morte whirrs down trailing
feathers like shroud garments.
Turns, her beak becomes fleshy lips.
She speaks lies in a language
I don't want to understand.
She holds up a mask to hide her skull.
A stiff white Venetian face,
almond spaces curved in gold.
Black holes in her head.
She is all brocade, lace, gauze
sequins and silver flowers.
She is all Carnival, insincere.
I attack her in silence.

Jenny Morris

Intruder

I wake just before five.
It is still dark – turn on the light,
go to the bathroom. On the way
I notice something brown next to the sink.

Ugh! A surprising mixture
of disgust, fear, and indignation rises.
What is it doing in my territory?
Let it go back where it belongs!

Five minutes later I look at it again.
It is not slimy, not even ugly,
its milk-chocolatey body covered
by skin with regular parallel ridges,

the front third lifted up; I feel –
although I can detect no features –
it's giving me a friendly, tentative grin
beneath those horns. This is imagination
gone too far.

Disgust has gone. Nevertheless
as I go back to bed, I have made up my mind:
tonight I must make sure
the plug sits firmly in its hole.

When I get up at seven, it has gone.

Alice Beer

The Death's Head Galliard

Arc, laser, fire and flare,
hearth, star and ice glow. None catch
this tinder dryback, burnt fireback black
between sockets, this sulk case –
nothing belies me, not light,
not the grave paced state step,
not the gloom of office. I will triple it
chromatic, fast as the spinning worm
mask it. My case at the crown court
is closed, the silk fee settled: now
my scale slides into the minor, on the wire
the rapid harmonics skip out of sight.

Ever yours, fondlings, dear ones,
your workhorse, bonehorse, your fancy.
I glide over gloom lakes cracking the time,
splash ashen waters, clout headlands,
fart like backfire down deep wells.
Night stalks my firework fingers,
blacks your workhouse, bonehouse.
I'm the hobby that grinds your days:
in three and in six, this side and that,
your caper, your shout, your show.

Pamela Coren

26

The Haunted House
(from *Nine Yorkshire Poems*)

That house over there,
That house is home to a ghost.
They've changed that house inside,
Raised ceilings and floors,
But the ghost still haunts his home,
Legs dangling through the ceiling,
Trunk and grey head advancing
On the upstairs carpet.

Ruth Silcock

No One

A voice in the orchard
when I was digging. *Here I am,*
hair and bone.
Don't hide me again!
One more waking, one more bite
of the apple, one more dance.
Don't cut me dead.

A cloud put out the sun. My spade
struck on stone.
No one.

M R Peacocke

Time Out

Where I am staying since the accident
they let you have one hour off
each anniversary. I've planned it all,
I'm going to have fun.

Rosie, my husband's second wife asleep
on our bed, same house, same room: Michael
was never blessed with much imagination.
He's a sound sleeper too.

I blow an icy breath into her face, also –
quite sotto voce – bloodcurdling whistles
in her ear. She's wide awake now.
Next: her feet.

I tickle them, go higher gradually; she lies
quite still, can't think what's happening.
I pinch her not too gently where it won't show.
Time's passing quickly.

Then for the throat: press, let go, repeat twice,
to finish, plonk my icy body on top hers.
Still no reaction, she's stiff with fright,
eyes open, hands tight fists.

On my way back I pass a man, unsteadily
making his way home from the club;
a few light kicks and he lies on the pavement,
my trademark whistles in his ears.

Slip in just before one. Wonder what Rosie
will tell her Michael over breakfast.
He'll say: Poor Rosie, what a horrid dream!
I'm always careful not to leave marks.

Alice Beer

Exploit

When, that February evening, a scuttling leaf
shape-shifted into a frog, to springheel
over the pavement, out to the thundering headlights
while we stood gawping,

flinching as it swerved and emerged by the breadth
of a webbed toe between giant wheels, still leaping,
passionate and elastic, towards the grassy
scents of water and sex

across lanes of traffic – it was you who scrambled
into the dazzle and roar, and after a teetering
moment scooped up the soft limbs, the pulsing
body, returning with it

to stare at its coppery eye and settle it back
on a rain-beaded bush behind *The Monkey's Forehead*
from which we walked away in the blustering dark
not daring to look behind us.

Christine Webb

Wordnurse

She's popping in
wearing a word mask
   round eyes slit mouth

trotting across
in patent word shoes
   neat word apron

Time to set up
a word drip Tap tap
   look for a vein

elbowing out
the blessed silence
   No words today

thank you   but Oh
she cries We'll have you
   as right as rain

I say No   please
don't change the dead bulbs
   I want my dark

but she's smiling
clipping new fuses
   to my eyeballs

plugging me in
jacking me alive
   Now then just a

little wordsip
(let's make sure nothing
   is understood)

                    M R Peacocke

Managers

She creates
the illusion of a tail,
tip waving
importantly over her head,

is gifted
with the psychology of

a pterodactyl.

Would not be out of place
in a medieval bestiary;

chimera
in a power suit,

basilisk rampant on fierce heels.

**

A touch of the gunslinger:

his need
to convey the skill to kill
has been achieved,
thin limbs, opaque face,
the way
he cuts a space in the room.

He walks like a weapon.

Not a warrior,
no artistry of sheen,
his ore is cold and clean
as competent steel;

his own mettle grows mean.

Isobel Thrilling

At the Art Gallery, a Woman

Dark things come out of me, she said
and opened her mouth
right there, next to the lemon poppyseed
muffins and chai teas,
parted her thin ribbed lips
and showed me her throat.
It was full of something
coiled. Leaning close to my face,
she rolled her eyes. Her laughter
rose between us on small black wings
leaving a dampness on my cheek.
Later, across the gallery
I saw her passing pamphlets
and brochures to visitors. Nothing dark
apparently, but high above in the rafters
there might have been movement.
She saw me watching
and winked.

Jude Goodwin

Revenant

That pigjawed god with his thick phallus
who strolled into the garden, glimming
about with snailshell eyes,
crowdark among a sprawl of stems (how
could I swear that I saw him?) snatching
at nerine lilies and cardoon heads
and dragging boughs of half-ripe damsons down –
gone, when I turned my head.

But she, pleading some task, has risen
abruptly to go in. That shudder;
that red weal on her neck...
How the season is changing! we'll say,
drawing the curtains, loath to remark
on the plum trees, barked and scored, bleeding
new resin, or where something has plundered
the bees' nest in the wall.

M R Peacocke

Cobaea scandens

These pods are time bombs
hanging off our front fence,
in every one a hundred seeds
just waiting to leap out.
People steal them, attracted
by huge flowers opening creamy green,
darkening in days to lilac, purple:
cups on saucers, homely
but beautiful in their way.
What they don't know
is how fast this thing grows: that
you can almost see the tendrils move
as the vine sprawls across the fence,
reaching for handhold after handhold,
then sweeping towards the house.
Leave the window open a crack
and it's in, slithering
across the floor, eager to explore
inside the airing cupboard
and under the fridge,
slipping up the stairs,
feeling its way into the bathroom,
nosing between the sheets.

Ruth Sharman

Robin

(from *Two Nannies*)

Pale, frail Robin,
White face, pointed chin,
Dark eyes and skinny legs –
What is wrong with him?

Is it his great big Nanny,
Overshadowing him?
Is it her bedtime stories?
Is that what's wrong with him?

She says that a sharp steel needle
Was lost below Robin's white skin
And it's travelling, travelling,
Until it finishes him.

Ruth Silcock

Secrets

Teddy
who has no eyes
no ears no mouth has seen
and heard everything   he tells
nothing

Gina Shaw

Not Suffering the Midnight Owl

Don't come near me, Mr. Owl,
with your hooter, your clock,
your creepy talents.
I don't want to know
about crop failure, plague, war,
about the loss of lawsuits.
Stuff your motorway crashes,
your lost children, your footsie index.

Your pinion feathers caress me
solicitously. I don't want to feel
the brown feathers and the white
tickling my ear. I can feel
my nose twitch in terror,
my legs shrink to the long splay feet
of the undergrowth, the leaf cover.

Turn your mad head away,
right round to the day you came from
when you stole the sun and ate it.
I see it bulge in your head,
swelling your eyes round the yellow point,
the arrow-slit where the barons shot my father
for running, man, for running.

Pamela Coren

The Real Bedtime Story

I'm the thing that's under your bed
to bite at tender night-time toes.
I'm not in any Disney films;
no little girlies' noxious squeaks
and nauseous frills disturb my rest.
You won't find me on nursery walls
nor caught in plush and gummed to death,
dissolved in slime from puking whelps.

I'm the worm that gripes old women
to yearn for young flesh and the itch
that sends the wolf to speak in tongues.
I'm the knife that hacks at heels,
the bloody smear on crystal slippers,
the hex in the apple. You need me.

Angela France

Hellhags & Changelings

Enter Sprite on a Rainy Night

We are battened down, the battering
at the windows won't relent. Inside
the house we do not trust the water.
Taps spit and shut. Hearts tick, awash

in all that fluid, awaiting action
of a more solid kind. Only the men,
cosy in the firelight, know to blow the foam
from their glasses and keep their voices low.

Upstairs it is big business, sweats and glow,
heated discussion. Electricity fumbles
at a window. It is a night
some of us have been waiting for.

It is allowed one jolly man with bag
to bound upstairs. A finger outlines
the rim of a glass. All around the house
persist the snags and rockets of the rain.

The woman splits out a child, sluices it
from its element, frothy, screw-faced
watersprite drawing voice as briny
and clear as a siren-song.

The women wipe and wash and snip and salve,
the white light of their fierce business
streaming into the night, filling the dark fields,
up to the very rafters of the pooling stars.

Diane Tang

41

Witch

Mine is the skill to straddle a ragwort stalk,
rise against the moon, stir the stars and skim
the chimneys prodding the sky at the end
of the land, or shift my shape to owl or hare
and arc across the moor.

Mine is the craft bought with the midnight touch,
nine-times, of the logan stone, and in church
with wine, the wafer saved to feed a toad,
and three times said 'Our father', end to start,
to woo the outside gods.

Mine are the charms to summon sudden storms
when rich ships ride the tide, shine lights
to warn of thrashing seas, bounce balls of fire
up carns or down the shafts and tunnels
lined with copper veins.

Mine is the gift to sail in a bladebone boat,
call down the wind or sell it to sailors: knots
on a thread to be unstrung, one for a breath,
two for a gale behind, three to blow
the vessel safely home.

Yours is the power to steal my strength
with an onion stuck with pins to pain my limbs,
a waxen manikin thrown into the flames,
a silver bullet, a shovelful of fire ...
if you should dare.

Gill Learner

Stepmother's Tale

He was a banded offer:
want him, get her too.
She grizzled for her sainted mother.

Three's a crowd. God knows I tried.
He didn't want the bother.
I took a course in parenting. She cried.

Drove me quite demented,
with her snow white, black and red.
I heard the rumours: *squatting in
a house with seven men.*
He blamed me, slept in the spare bed.

Even the mirror lied. The fairest. *She.*
You bet I wished her ill.
The rest you know about: the fatal fruit,
the glass box on the hill.

Ann Alexander

Landed

She returns from the sea with a boy child;
sand-coloured, quartz eyed.
She says his name is Jack, plants their home
in the centre of the land. She dresses him
in brown and green, guides his frond-soft
fingers to push seeds into earth, rocks him
from his back-forth rushing with stories
of mountains and plains;

                    of high, dry, places.

She banishes waves from the house; changes
his alphabet: fish to fowl, shark to sheep.
His hair floats around his head, catches
the sun in winks of light, won't stay down
when she brushes it. She strokes oil
on his skin where it cracks, dry; tutors
the sibilant lisp from his speech.
    She can't meet his pebble gaze
    when he salts his drink of water.

Angela France

44

Dark of the Moon

Tonight she is an old bag
the moon. Pointed hat
hidden by rain clouds
she stumbles over the sky's
debris.

Looking for a dirty doorway
shining on Soho
on her back legs akimbo
those were the days
remembering
golden hearted whores
weeping blood onto cobbles
now chrome and matt black.

Who sees her behind glass
behind bars in Brixton
carrying her light up the hill
in baskets from the market
to those dark courtyards
full of notices and grim puddles.

Ragged wolves in the park
howl at her shining face
dull railings, white canal, litter.
No Rocky Mountains
under the skin.
She flaunts her marvels
mapped and mysterious.

Into the bright night waters
of the river she dives skinny dip
teeth rigid at rivals
only the sky notices cold
for a moment her absence.
Deep dazzled she
gulps down unnecessary
party boats, ducks on the loose.

Looming risible
under Hungerford Bridge
broom invisible she sweeps
all the jewels of the river
onto her neck.

Berta Freistadt

Holy Innocents

Late on Holy Innocents came the crying.
We opened the door an inch to find
the thing curled like, yet not quite like, a kitten,
as if dropped new-born in the icy yard.
We tempted it with cow's, then sheep's milk,
until Anna giggling expressed milk into a spoon
which it lapped eagerly. We put it with the cat
against the cold and went to bed.
Only to stop suddenly. No earthly noise.
Frozen we ventured down the stairs to see it
huge and black crouching with eyes like passion
in the dark. I ran to the door and threw it open.
'Go' I shouted as the wind blew snow and litter
from the farmyard back into the kitchen.
She bent over the cat and cried out
pointing to the place its throat had been.

Marianne Burton

Jadis

Cas digests her Christmas dinner,
hands round the chocolates. For herself
prefers to savour just one small
piece of organic fudge; ponders

how our genetic history
nudges us to feast on butter
and sugar, to lay down stores in
the body's own larder; rations

for secret younger selves frantic
to survive long ice-age winters.
As she chews the last chunk she feels
a touch on her neck. Far too cold.

She's re-read the book, knows that dead
white fingerprint. Jadis: witch who's
moved on from doling out Turkish
Delight. Instead she cajoles with

a huge plasma TV left on
stand-by; a school-run SUV;
skiing in Dubai. Cas flinches
from the icy breath of Jadis

who can hardly wait, whose hands itch
to stab the Gulf Stream's 'OFF' button,
to shroud all the British Isles in
shadow – lands adrift under deep

mounds of snow; to pack soft throats with
remaindered delight: a brittle
toffee – thick-layered glacier
ice ages past its sell-by date.

Hilary J Murray

47

Goldilocks

After that startled awakening and chase through the woods
bears lumbered almost nightly
into her dreams

but by the time she married, she couldn't remember
why even the smell of porridge
could scald her tongue.

She has a baby now, and her broken sleep is invaded
by bears again – their coarse dark fur
smelling of resin and fungus.

Sometimes she wakes with honey in her throat
hands as cumbersome as boxing gloves
flat white nails thickened to ebony.

When she slides from the bed
it seems natural as breathing
to pad across the carpet on all fours.

Grey light seeps through loosely woven
nursery rhymes. She unravels undertones of
talcum powder, sweat-damp hair

and hints of her own milk on sleeping breath.
Her baby. Is he hers? He seems so
separate

folded in on his unblemished self
as though he's tumbled through a crack in time
and she can't touch him.

Christine Coleman

View from the Crossroads

When the pain and the rope didn't matter any more, I could see
how knowledge and sight had brought me here, not dancing
naked at night, for I am too fond of comfort to chill, skyclad,
under a cold moon and nightshade oil is foul stuff that stings.

Charges were laid of curses, of curdled milk and sick
cows, of consorting with he they won't name. I don't see
any sense in spoiling milk I may have to buy, and I've never
met a man I'd lie for, so one that's half goat won't bend me.

Herb-lore and healing are a way to live for a plain woman,
a way to breathe and a way to hold the gates of comings
and goings. We see that the greatest begin face down
in a woman's shit, the holy still puke and grizzle as babes.

In the end, my crime is this: that I know the long bones
of a great man are the same to wash and lay out as those
under a pauper's flesh, and that I see the pox on the priest's
pizzle, the stains of sin under the rich man's cloth.

Angela France

From the Void
(on Uccello's *St George and the Dragon*, National Gallery)

O you
who have divided the waters
who have ridden the storm
hurling your thunderbolts
all you roaring boys
of the resurrection
dragon-slayers
who boast bringing order
to chaos

Hear me

Your spears will not enter
the core of the labyrinth
nor your harpoons the heart
of Leviathan
your sword and your lance
will be lost
in the cave of the chimera
and will fall   slowly spinning
into the open mouth
of hell

Remember this

Chaos
is merely an arrangement
you do not understand

Joy Howard

This Poem has Nothing to do with Me

It cannot wait to rise up from the page
and denounce me, to claim it has never so much
as been seen with me.

All my dreams and disasters are nothing to this poem.
It doesn't care about my ear, my backache,
my bad eyes. It only wants out of my hands.

It tries to convince me it is time
to make its own way, its own mistakes.
I would like to be able to say

there will always be somewhere
for it to come home to
but quite honestly, I don't care for it.

It doesn't look like me. It is, to be blunt,
very ugly. I am ashamed of its rough accent,
the things that it says,

how it holds up its filthiest laundry
for all to examine. I can't think where
it picked up its language, its half-baked ways

of looking at things.
I don't know what this poem is anymore
and frankly I'm beginning not to care.

Though sometimes I'm moved to remember
the hopeful beginnings, the first bright days.
Those new eyes turned on me.

It looks at me now
with no sign of affection or recognition.
It has nothing of my kindly disposition.

It is driving me to distraction
with its constant demands for attention,
its casual malice; its lewd suggestions.

I wanted to make something beautiful.
Instead, I got this.

I wake with its baleful face on my pillow,
and all night,
its spiteful little elbows in my back.

I was assured that
despite all its faults I would love it.
But it leaves me cold.

I was told very soon
I would forget all the pain,
Would try for another.

Never.

Clare Shaw

The Expert

Professional smile:

blue gaze freezes a path
five metres
ahead of her track.

Walls stiffen,
pictures turn pale.

She has come to mould us,
we are
her new ingredients.

She cuts out our lives
like pastry,
batches of time
to be served on the board,

work fodder,

devoured and
consumed like a plate of scones.

Isobel Thrilling

A Taste of Ginger

Gretel liked older women:
she weakened for grey hair, lines
around piercing eyes and the decayed
confidence to grasp where they hunger.

She'd found some reason
in therapy; in reconciling
sibling rivalry with her inner
child; but liver spots, or a bent
knuckle still captivated her notice
with a thrill she couldn't name.

Gretel watched her brother
deny the dark, and the time lost:
watched him grow diamond
hard and caged by their past.
She swore that she'd stay open
to her future.

      Yet watching him
made her shiver, as if memory
were a snap of ginger on her tongue.
She knew she could never stop
searching for the ravenous desire
that an older woman had
once shone at him.

Angela France

Black Sheep
(after a picture by Paula Rego)

Three bags full I ordered.
Got the number from the Yellow Pages—
'Black Sheep Enterprises'. He sounded
ever so nice on the phone.
When could he deliver? I said
the afternoon'd be fine.

Well I thought it was the devil:
black horns coiled like ammonites.
But there was something about him.
I stashed the wool away right quick,
let my red face cool.

And now my fingers work
a living fleece, one cloven foot
lost in the folds of my full skirt.

My little one is coming down the lane.
His days of nursery rhymes are numbered.

Kathryn Daszkiewicz

Sirens' Song

Tie   tie Ulysses
the knots that hold you fast
cling   cling to the rigging
hold   hold to the mast

Play   play you wavelets
smile to the sky above
laugh   laugh at the sailors
who fear to be lost for love

We kiss   we kiss the salt spray
from our siren lips as we sing
then turn   turn and leave you
to the sport of the green sea king

Joy Howard

Scarlet Woman

Rose Madder lives in a room of reds.
Her hangings, ceilings stained with blood:
gore crimson, claret, carmine shades
and coral carpets, rufous rugs.
Soft cushions toned in cochineals
and deep vermilions glow by lamps
which shine with wine and ruby glass.
Here's rich womb warmth and sanguine love.

Jenny Morris

Witchcraft

Hecate, arch-witch of Witchery;
Circe, harsh Bewitchery;
Medusa, stony Bitchery;
Clotho, fateful Stitchery;
Cleopatra, fickle Ditchery,
Aphrodite – Seven Year Itchery.

Gill McEvoy

You Have Been Warned

The Perils of Ageing

Faster and faster the sledge travels over the snow,
Louder and louder the wolves are howling – we know
That we'll have to throw somebody out – and while the
       wolves feed
We can whip up the horses – our only hope is their speed.

But the night is still dark and our horses are tired and we hear
The distant howling of wolves once again coming near
And someone else must be thrown to the wolves – we all
      know
That soon it will be our turn to be flung on the snow.

Ruth Silcock

It's the Threat that Counts

You want to hear an old lady talk for hours
about her blemished skin?

No, that's why I didn't write this poem
but take care. I was far younger then.

Anne Stewart

61

I, the Sea

The bony face of the moon hangs above me
with unseen hands as huge as the earth
she hauls on her ropes
compels my waters

Joyous and savage in my obedience
I rise towards her
I celebrate her queenship with my colours –
my steel, my sand, my glaucous marbles
my clouded lion-coloured glass

I rise towards her
with my giant curves
my molten architecture
my scrolling and spiralling
my roaring revolutions

We come together, the moon and I
with terrible laughter
we eat the rocks, the shingle, the sand
we grind it small

Christine Webb

Curse

that the next doorhandle you turn
steals your entire body's sense of touch;

that the next flower you scent
stuffs your sinuses with burning rubber – forever;

that at the next sip of tea you take
your tastebuds dissolve to acid slush;

that at the next touch of your toothbrush,
your tongue grows to 6 metres –

with the musculature
of a burst earthworm;

that the next time you look at your watch
that will be all you ever see from then on –

counting down the seconds,
of only ever seeing your watch;

and then, that you get absolutely
everything you want in life,

and still hate it.

Char March

When All You Need's a Knife

It was not-love at first sight.
Older, and none too handsome,
but he was the man, all right.
A man to strike a deal with.

Some said she could have had any man
but, being in no condition,
she whittled a hasty plan
and made the opening gambit.

Too much drowned without waving,
failure was no option.
Too much in need of saving,
efficiency was the key.

Witnesses might have called it rude.
It certainly wasn't pretty.
Ten minutes, he was hooked, lined and screwed.
She made a mental note about machetes.

Anne Stewart

Discretion

So when you bawl and stamp your feet at me
and I retreat, you must think it's from fear.
You're right. I wanted to live neighbourly
but all you seem to know is snarl and jeer.

I don't know what you got so mad about
although I know it isn't only me
you aim it at, because I've heard you shout
at window cleaners, dogs, your family.

The trouble is I'm not the little mouse
you'd like, and if I start on you one day
I might not stop, so I go in the house
before you're dead and I get locked away.

It's not the way you rage that makes me wary.
It's what I want to do to you that's scary.

Gina Shaw

Rebecca
(from *Two Nannies*)

'Don't walk with one foot on the pavement and one in
       the gutter –
Just look at Rebecca –
A car ran over her foot that was in the gutter,
And see how it's wrecked her –
You're sorry now, but it's what you deserved,
You foolish Rebecca.'

Ruth Silcock

Enchanter's Nightshade
(from *The Observer's Book of Wild Flowers*)

Along the glades of damp woods
beside the thickets and undergrowths

be found

tall, slender, faintly toothed
studded with pellucid dots
an egg shaped fruit covered with hooked bristles

Do not hold up to the light

Joy Howard

Waterlilies

Few things achieve
the immaculate whiteness
of these waterstars

drawn by a child
who thinks of sky-stars
as stemless flowers

and has laid them here
to float among dragonflies
and waterboatmen

on a surface that reflects
trees, leaves and lilies
but gives nothing away

of that other world,
swollen stems reaching down
through darkness to where

spider eggs are hatching,
caddis grubs are building
homes from sticks and stones,

and if you've delved
into that darkness,
you'll know the soft, cold ooze

that sneaks between your toes
as you step in, and how,
as you thrash to free yourself,

those supple roots wrap
insistently around your legs,
slippery as eels.

Ruth Sharman

Accident of Birth

The family tree can hold you fast
with ties of guilt or love or pride.
Opprobrium may haunt its past
but bonds of blood are sanctified.
Though you may choose your friends with care,
in kith and kin you have no choice.
Regarding them it may be rare
you find a reason to rejoice.
Yes, you can run away from home,
divorce your parents if you like,
escape from relatives and roam –
until you find you are alike.
Those inbred traits will bind you fast.
When you were made the die was cast.

Jenny Morris

Portrait

She conjures
confectionery of chatter,

words in candy-colours
cakes and sweets.

A porcelain person:

cocks her smile
like a little finger above a cup.

Beware
the glaze in conversation;

pearl-handled knife beneath

Isobel Thrilling

Monday Morning

ice at the station

jackdaw patrols the white line
at the edge of the platform

flops down
to check the rails

all the while eyeing you
eyeing you

as though he knows something
as though he knows

you shiver

Gina Shaw

Beware of the Dog

In the Chumchomping, leghumping,
blindleading, arselicking, shepherding,
heelwalking, lift-up-your-paw
and shake-hands drooling heart
of a slavering slave of a dog –

curls what's left of the gene
of the Little Red
can'tseethewoodforthe

Wolf. And it wants letting out.

Ann Alexander

Separating the Sheep from the Goats

The sheep don't learn
Especially in Spring
They decorate
The flat green field
Beyond the railway line
With lambs
Unlikely, woolly white
As we, in fact, expect of them
But they don't ever learn.

Each night
The train goes by
And every night
They run away from it
Surprised and terrified
Each time
It is a different train
A different, timeless time
For them
Because they never learn

Unlike the brown-backed goats
Who graze the steep
Embankment just above
the tracks.
Some turn towards the train
Their eyes like signals.
Most, however,
Measure-up the sheep
Their eyes all wrong
Black upright slits, like knives.

J A Priestman

Let's Get This Straight

It's not "being positive"
that gets you through. No,

it's something grittier – sharp, capable of hurt:
it would have you grabbing the very last crumb
from under your best friend's nose,
it's savage, stubborn, it's made of steel –
if you were in business the whole world
would hate your guts. So,

the next person to come along and say
"Think positive" and all that sort of crap
will get it right between the eyes.
For I'm a hard woman now:
I am diamond, carborundum,
and I wipe out fools.

Gill McEvoy

Shape Shifting

Becoming a Seal

Becoming a seal takes dedication.
I've time for little else now
what with days in snack bars
accumulating layer on layer of flab
and evenings stretched out in the bath
holding my breath under water.

Night swells with dreams of blubber
light as airships, supple and strong
as branches of willow. Sometimes I lurk
by plastic ponds in garden centres.
After a little practice, Koi carp
slip down smoothly as noodles.

My place of pilgrimage is Blakeney Point.
Those massive bolster shapes basking
on sandbanks barely glance towards me
as I wriggle inch by inch a little closer.
Now that I've tuned in to their grunts and barks
I understand their conversations.

Lately I've noticed changes in my skin –
it's thicker now and turning mottled grey.
Each plunging struggle against
North Sea tides creates a tingling glow
though I still have to coat myself with grease
before I slide into the waves.

When my legs have fused together
they'll propel me faster. I'll have no need
for arms – the sinuous seals caress
from head to tail. Soon I will smell
as they do. They'll nuzzle me gently
gliding around me along the sea-bed.

Christine Coleman

Re-growing Pinions

She's had anal sex
and rather liked it.
She scoffs baby-new potatoes,
that you scorned, they squeak
round her teeth like wax eyes.
She lugs in occasional armfuls
of those lilies that made you choke.

On Sunday mornings there is
no Radio 2. She kayaks and
has buried the cat you left –
he was dead, just.
She sucks tuna straight
from the tin; has never made
another Swiss roll; took E
for her 56th; sings Bessie Smith
on the loo – the door never shut.

The herpes you gave her
erupts every few months
but now she doesn't interrogate
the steamed mirror with panda
eyes – she swallows Lysine,
is careful of her nut intake.

(Pinions are the flight feathers that owners cut off on their
ornamental birds to prevent them flying away.)

Char March

The Unmade Girl

Remember Rackets? She
was there, a kind of unfinished
thing, an unmade girl. Slipping
darkly round the edges
of the room, taking the shadows
with her. Was she always
in black? Black legs, shirt,
black eyes and hair? Corners
whispered as she went by and
liquid in glasses shivered
in apprehension of a thunderstorm.
Sometimes empty chairs tipped
silently backwards into the empty
hole in the ground when it
cracked open as she passed. Now
she teaches children, smiles
and drives a car. She has
a clever woman for a lover
and crosses the room
by the shortest route. But I
remember that unmade girl
and I know the corners do too.
They moved to a place near her
when Rackets had to be rebuilt.

Berta Freistadt

Cave Rescue

She does not want to escape
and no amount of coaxing
will tempt her.
Whatever made you think
it was possible?

This is the one way out, see,
where the people are, and the air.
But calling will only scare her.
Who knows what your fingers look like
from there, or your face?

She won't eat, everyone knows that.
For every crumb you offer her,
she shuffles further back.
With the best will in the world
she can't last in there another week.

When they come for her
with their bright lights and their anecdotes,
their impossibly noisy dogs,
she'll be off –
retreating through cracks

where no grown man could enter,
through caverns the size of cathedrals
cluttered with rock, deep
into unnamed seas, over black forests
laid down in coal.

here is a fish is an arrow
here is a pot is a bracelet a bone

She won't know you anymore.
She's losing her manners,
her language, her shoes.
Her memory, the knee of her trousers –
it's all coming away.

You've warned them.
But no-one believes a word.

Clare Shaw

When I Was Twelve

When I was twelve, and crying,
I found that tears were salty,
I found that tears could make rainbows
If I blurred my eyes.
Suddenly, here was science,
Also, here was creation –
I tried to cry again,
To recover the world.

Ruth Silcock

Sisterwrite

See me walking down
Upper Street:
Windy winter sunlight
pouring, hissing, through
impassive me. But inside
every step, a thousand
sparkling arabesques.
Every swing of the arms
a buck and a wing.
Snap. Stonefaced.
I've done it.
Persephone has bought
two glowing ears of wheat
to take down into the
marital hades.
Just two thin iconoclastic
books of verse.
But now, Persephone knows
where the cornucopia lives.
She no longer eats from
Pluto's hand.
Is she getting ready to
bite it?

Barbara Burford

Down to the Wood

The table has grown smug. It smirks
at her, winks in the lamplight
as she lifts her fork.

It came with the house: dead wood
wedging itself between them, her
back, closer to the wall each

year as he inserts another leaf.
Mahogany. She hears it settle
dreaming of forest.

Sometimes she hushes it with damask,
the way a cloth drapes silence
over a parrot's cage.

The fabric slides onto the floor, letting
the table hold her hands and face
in its deep sheen.

She's lost her appetite for balanced
meals on a polished surface. She'll
forage in the wood,

lips and fingers grained with
blackberry and juniper, no table
but the tawny floor of leaves.

Christine Coleman

This Long Journey

This long journey.
It's all been worth it
but where is the money

the studio
the room of one's own
and the jeep?

How is it progressing?
Step behind the curtain please.
This won't hurt a bit.

I have muttered and sworn.
For days I have put myself
in the past tense,

unable to bracket myself
with the best of them.
My tennis arm writing,

calling the shots
from my dusty brain.
What cowers in its attic,

senseless and dull,
that I can midwife, faceless
and angry, into the light?

Joanna Ezekiel

All the virgins have come in

and taken up their places in the museum
on glass shelves,
in long rows,
one after the other, after the other.

Each has a little boy baby, each achieves
therefore, what women
should,
lucky, lucky long-skirted virgins.

From the chunky, rough hewn twelfth
century, to
the roccoco,
smiling or weeping they seem comfortable

in their borrowed power from god
and the master carver,
armies
of them stuffed with a piquant male

fantasy of prayer. Look over your shoulder
at all the tortured
Christs,
their sufferings so elegantly drawn, as if

suffering is the dandyish option, an elite
occupation. Then
quickly,
turn back to the virgins. Was that a foot withdrawn

under a cloak? Is that ineffable smile a tinge
ironic? See, that one-
there,
I swear she spanked Him – and that one

cries real tears of fury and frustration
over her dead
son's
wasted breath. An escaped smile, a small, weary

hint of reality in lip or cheek, even the man
with the chisel, dreaming
of Jesus
can't negate the power of all the virgins coming in.

Kate Foley

The Dress

I wandered through a mansion in my dream
where countless dresses hung from countless rails.
Some were made of velvet, some of silk,
chenille or lace, and some were filmy veils
that slipped beneath my fingertips, soft
and shimmering in shades of white and cream.

I chose one and my husband helped me in.
In cut and shape it differed from the rest,
tapering to a mermaid's tail, its neck
revealing curves I lacked in life.
       The dress
he hooked me into was my wedding dress,
and it was black and fitted like a skin.

Ruth Sharman

The Mermaids of Atlantis Speak

Our father Neptune banged his stave three times:
the notes his throat made, long as ropes,
pulled the city under—if we'd refused,
we'd have been sent to try our luck on land.

By day, we squirm our emerald tails past
scattered bones and tumbled cooking pots.
The eyes of skulls are plankton caves.
With every hour, the pillars weep more dust.

We won't stay here by night. We know of sharks
that trail a stench we're scared to name.
The city swarms with echoes. Far beyond,
neon jellyfish pulse upward, searching.

Joanna Ezekiel

Bog Lady

I have come out of the peat to this white place,
to show my burnished skin, my tufts of ginger hair –
dreadlocked, beaded, stiff with dirt.

I was a stranger in that other time, lost on the tracks
that snake the wet. I crossed their boundary, and so
they took me, withy-bound, to meet my four slow deaths.

Since then I've slept and slept. I am Persephone,
dragged out of hell, reeking with different rules
which I must now forget. And learn instead

the ways of drying air, hushed tongues, the shrink
from difference, laws of other and strange.
What's left curls in disarray. I am in no man's land.

They found six seeds inside my gut. They speculate.
A wet place waits, bordering our worlds,
where they will float me soon
to meet another kind of death.

Ann Alexander

Metamorphosis

First came a taste for meat
and odd bursts of irritation
like an itch along the spine.

Then she lost her urge to speak.
She'd curl up in the back room,
whole days at a time,

and at night she'd sleep-walk
through the house, nudging
at the windows and doors,

lifting her face to the draughts,
listening to a wood louse
scratching under the apple bark.

She wondered at sofas and knives,
and no longer knew the meaning
of *milk* or the colour red,

what *hot* was and *cold*, and *nice*,
why some things shone and some
were dark, and why the baby cried.

Ruth Sharman

The Roses

'Do you know where he is?' she asked the roses.

The Snow Queen

Touch our heads, they are so pretty.
We are your friends. Who else would go
eyeless under the earth for you?
There are gas pockets and rocks there.

We tasted all the corpses root to root,
strapped and padded with cotton wadding,
wearing wedding dresses, tied with string,
the firm ones, the green, the liquid ones.

Everywhere we touched and tasted
asking 'is this Kay?'
we tasted the sex to see if it was boy
we tasted the limbs to see if it was child
we tasted residue to see how long dead.
He would not have been long dead.

Most are old or babies.
The babies are waxy and sour,
the old are soft and easy to palpate.

We stretch, distend towards food,
know all the mulched places.
News shoots straight through our network.
He is not here yet or we would know,
would offer you the petals he has grown.

Marianne Burton

Orchard Plainsong

The sun finally hits the crack in the corner of the window,
beams a sliver of rainbow to chime on the wall
and Mary knows it's time to mix sugar water. She leaves
the house's petty demands and glides to the orchard.
She takes care to move slowly, resisting the urge to run,
averting her eyes from the lascivious shirts and underwear billowing
on the line. She sings hymns under her breath while she lifts the hive lid,
whispers to the queen *Come to Mary – it's our time.* She settles
on Mary's breast and, as the workers cluster, Mary stands
with her hands out, palms turned up. Bees gather over her chest
and neck, spread over her face. She is sure of feeling every tiny foot
telegraphing obeisance, certain of their love. Her eyes open wide
as she feels a rare sting and she smiles, nods
in acknowledgement of sacrifice.

Angela France

Persephone

At the corner of the eye. The corner of the lane.
Dark hair plastering her cheek. The skin of her arms
peaky cold. (April, and still no warmth
in the white sun.) Skimping shirt. She looks away,
chewing. It's like a film,
flashback to the mother (fleshy but still handsome)
abandoning everything for the search, distraught,
and such a winter. Five months, the girl turns up,
stows in her cheek whatever it is,
braces herself for kisses,
regular meals, the dressing of her hair. All summer
she looks sheepishly happy, her cheeks almost rosy.
She'll talk about clothes at times, express
preferences, but her eyes are tinged
with nettleroot yellow. You can tell
it won't last. She's bound to abscond. Submitting
once more to the gaze that knows her and mocks her,
to his greed and neglect, will be like downing
the first drink after an age
of abstinence. Nothing could be worse.
Nothing could be better.

M R Peacocke

Red

Now that it's over
the nightmare of white skirts
the careful sleeping in other
people's sheets
flowers flowers blooming
I've taken to drinking red wine
swirling the last dark mouthful
in the clear glass.

Only some wines quite catch that
black brown watery tone of red
that half forgotten colour
most are too deep too blue
and I can almost taste the smell
that tang of iron
the pain they call dragging

no word for the heavy damp lump
between the chafed thighs
of a twelve year old
I lay in the school sick room
wondering
about being a woman
I walked down the corridor
worrying about odour.

Ballet class
there were laughable incidents
but finally when the end was near
I clung on to pitiful flow
thinking it made me who I was.

Now that it's over
flowers flowers blooming
I'm surprised
that I'm a woman still.

Berta Freistadt

Goddesses

They belong to their faces
as only those
who've become the landscape of their skins,
belong.

They belong to their breasts,
reach casually into their bras,
feed peevish businessmen,
crying children, a parcel of nuns,
the odd dictator.

Often asked for forgiveness
or other impossible things,
and petitioners steadily,
as a gift.
No return is asked
or expected.

They belong to their bellies,
relish a digestif of sly chuckles,
and fat peals of laughter,
dirty as soapsuds when a job is done.
Appetite, old friend, is known biblically,
met in the pleasure of pleasing.

They belong to their wombs,
only as those who are sure
the seed case is not the seed
and the root hair not the soil.

Ordinary as a Tesco tillroll,
they belong to their deaths

as utterly as fading comes
and one collapsing star feeds another.

Fortunately,
there are very many more of them than you think.

Kate Foley

New Fruit

In the last knockings of the evening sun
Eve drinks Calvados. Elsewhere in her life
She has played muse and mistress, bitch and wife.
Now all that gunpoint gamesmanship is done.
She loves the garden at this time of day.
Raising her third glass up to God, she grins;
If this is her come-uppance for her sins
It's worth a little angst along the way.
A fourth. Again the cork's slow squeaky kiss.
If, as the liquor tempts her to believe,
The Lord has one more Adam up His sleeve
He's going to have to take her as she is –
Out in the garden in a dressing-gown
Breathing old apples as the sun goes down.

Ann Drysdale

And Another Thing...

You Took My Space

You took my space
and when I protested
(too politely)
'It's Disabled Parking'
you snarled 'Too many
bloody Disabled
Spaces' and sped away
into Marks & Spencer's.

In Marks & Spencer's
nothing will fit you
the assistants sneer
as you root through the knickers
laughter follows you
down all the aisles
the food counters
are full of spinach
and frozen cod heads
eyeing you glassily
huge queues snake
back from the checkouts
the cashiers go on strike
a hoaxer shouts Fire
the building is evacuated
someone else's child
is sick in your handbag
and out in the car park
a delivery lorry
has crushed your car
to a dense metal cowpat
before blocking the exit.

Be my guest, madam.

Christine Webb

Message

Dear both
Eileen called. You were out.
Wonder why? Ha-ha.
I have left the banjo in the fridge
And scraped off most of the cheesecake.
The woman was seeing red.
Jesus. I was scared I don't mind telling you.
And her plaster cast only just off on the
Thursday.

She says — "I see Paddy McGintey is away back to
His old she-goat." (Apparently, that's you Sinead.)
Ha-double-ha.
And why no rent left for me in usual place,
While I think of same??
No-bloody-ha-at-all-ha.
Am living on fresh-air and ciggies here.
Can you not have some decency?
Did I not get you the phone number of
Christy Moore's ex-brother-in-law?

Anyway. Eileen says she'll see both of you in hell
Before the band's left to youse two's
Cheating bastards. And no,
I don't know where she got the goat.
He only answers to "Will you move your arse ye eejut,
Before I move it for ye."
I'm lying. He answers to bugger all.
Keep your frigging paws off that last piece of cheesecake.
See you in hell — yours (the other cheating bastard)
Eithne Cecilia Cavanagh, your
Ever loving landlady.

Helen Burke

Regarding Delivery

Of course, there's no way we can guarantee
how long. The maker, normally a man,
will always believe his goods are perfect
on leaving. Difficulty may occur
in transportation, whether at departure
(particularly if the way is blocked
or when the fuel gauge is low), in transit
(the carrier may accidentally shed
the load) and even at delivery
(the packaging may skew, the goods may slip -
adopting such a difficult position
that the contractor has to use a tool
to grasp protruding parts). The cost of damage
is to be borne by the recipient.

Ruth O'Callaghan

Baker Street Station

Pigeons think it's theirs.
They generously allow trains
and humans its use.

Alice Beer

This Christmas, the Spirit is Rum

I'd like to say something new about Christmas
but it's all been said before

I wanted to be confident and decisive about it
but now I'm not sure

I'm not sure if I want to put out the Christmas tree,
the dinner

hang the lights, drop the tinsel, stuff the turkey.
And carol singers —

there are packs of ferocious carol singers
out on the hunt

I don't want anything this Christmas
I don't want

I hope you've had as good a year as mine
and next is one to match it

Ah, Christmas. Time to bring the family round
and bury the hatchet.

Anne Stewart

The Obituary

When you read about his life,
that kindly, half-blind precis;
four hundred weasel words, on
the easy passage through the famous school,
the glittering career,
his wit and wisdom, how he was
so admired by other men,

And at the very end you read
In 1953 he married Muriel,
one daughter, and one son survive –

Oh, Muriel, his true and loving wife,
what was your contribution to this life?

History should record:
In 1953 he was
rescued by a woman, who
in spite of all his triumphs
saw potential in him, nursed him through
all his self-doubt, all those infidelities,
the endless drinking bouts, persuaded him
he could make something of himself.
Stand up, girl – take a bow!

Don't hold your breath, Muriel.

Ann Alexander

Martha

(from 'Gospel Truths')

I was elbow-deep in grease. That lamb
(in a herb crust) doesn't exactly cook
itself. And there's a pan to scour after.
Then the home-made bread, bitterleaf salad
(lightly dressed with oil) not to mention
figs, plums, apricots, almonds and a couple
of bottles of wine. I didn't notice him
(or anyone) refusing second helpings
nor minding me dodging about with dishes,
spooning gravy, cutting extra bread.
After dinner, there's our Mary sitting
literally at his feet – he has the one
comfortable chair, she's hunched on a cushion
drinking it all in. I'm doing a quick sweep
round the kitchen, hoping to get back to the chat
half listening to them while I go on stacking
pots. Then here he is in the doorway:
'Mary's made the best choice,' he says.
I stare. Is this a joke? My good lamb
hardly out of his mouth, beard stained with gravy:
'You should prioritise more. Don't spend so long
in the kitchen.' And he's on his way,
picking a thread of meat from his teeth. God.

Christine Webb

Telephone Call

Your voice sounds eager
after so many years.
Can we meet? you ask,
reeling off places and dates.

Having a pen but no paper,
I put it all down on my leg:
first on my kneecap; you talk
up to my thigh.

Later I wash it off
and it's quickly gone:
some water, a little soap.
Look, it has left no mark.

Gerda Mayer

To Those Who Love Me

I listed fifty reasons not to die.
The only three that stood alone were you.
I crossed out forty five that wouldn't do, but,
because one day I'm likely to need lies,
I only pencilled out the other two.

Anne Stewart

Your Letter Did Not Come Today

I recognized it at once –
the way it failed to make
its usual belly-flop
down onto the mat,
every unwritten
flourish and curlicue
in blue-black Stephenson's
on the absent grey weave
of Conqueror's Smooth Satin
the faintest smear of saliva
which should have been
where, oddly enough,
a first-class stamp wasn't,
the trace of your after-shave –
spice and sandalwood,
that somehow eluded me –
and if only you had seen
how eagerly I didn't
tear open the envelope,
how easily I was seduced
by every ardent word
not found there, and how,
above all, I was entranced
with the way you'd added
those seven sweet
non-existent kisses.

Angela Kirby

Lunch Date

I asked him if he read
and he said he was trying to give it up.
I asked him why and he replied
that it was nice *handling* books,
the covers, the titles, the blurbs
but you always felt you had to *buy* one.
I said why not and he laughed.
Well, what would you *do* with it?

He asked if I was going shopping,
said he couldn't resist all those sales
and I said I might browse in a bookshop.
You know where you are with a book,
there's always one that fits,
they don't pinch in awkward places
and when you get them home
they still suit you. I let him pay.

Carole Bromley

Infection

She says she has
a chest infection. She
will not come near me
nor give me the customary
kiss. 'Shabat shalom.'
In the service she looks
in ecstasy, eyes shut
singing the Barekhu. And I wonder
which part of her cleavage
we could call her chest.
In that T-shirt her breasts
are certainly infectious.

Berta Freistadt

Unrequited – a Haiku

Always on my mind
and never where I want you
into my body

Joy Howard

Charles Kingsley's Saying

When I was young they told me all the time,
'Be good, sweet maid, and let who can be clever.'
To quote this line was a misguided crime.
I wanted to be bright. But good? God, never!

Jenny Morris

I will not shout

even though I'm wearing
sandals and a cream dress,
and some sonova dung-brained
Beamer driver has spotted
beside the bus stop
the only puddle between
here and the Atlantic
and done a quick swerve
to spatter the muck all over me
as punishment for being ugly
or twice his age or simply
belonging to that half
the human race he thinks
he's better than

no I will not shout

nor stick two fingers
in the air nor
let the smile slip
from my morning   I wish
I had a bottle of acid
to splash his perfect bodywork
I wish I could even the score
with a vicious scrape of my keys
along his blood red paint
but he's gone before the drops
or the thoughts have settled
so I'll let dirty water
wreak my vengeance
eating away at his undercarriage
till one day it rusts and all
his nuts and bolts drop off

Gina Shaw

109

Life is too Short to be Small

Dead give away, that 'good evening'.
I wonder where Mr. Alh sdlkfj lives?
I can just see him, sitting over a pint
with his cronies, bdlzo, Buck Hildebrandt,
and clyde smole feeling smug he's got past
the server, under the wire of the spam filter,
avoiding the junk mail box by the simple trick
of masquerading as a salesman, a friend,
a well-wisher. He must get the same kicks
as a flasher undoing his flies,
a heavy breather suddenly telling you
he'd like to fuck you right now.
I'm sure there's a way of blocking
all messages containing the word *penis*
but I'm damned if I can work out how.

Carole Bromley

An After-taste of Salt

Men, they never know what they want –
at first they can't get enough of us,
our phosphorescent breasts,
the way our bodies flicker in the dark,
the sequined flick of our tails,
that risky, salt-aftertaste of anchovies
and seaweed, and us being always
a little ahead of them somewhere,
way out beyond their bowsprits,

oh, they swear then we'll be mistress
of their hearts, queen of their hearth
and home, no jewel too rare for us,
we shall toil not, neither shall we spin –
and occasionally we believe them,
tell ourselves it might be worth a shot

but once they have us ashore,
when the shine and novelty wear off,
they don't know what to make of us,
so stay out late or stare into the fire,
take to drink, ignore us, wish
they had thrown us back
while the women cross themselves,
draw in their skirts, walk
on the other side of the road
and teach the children to catcall,
to jeer that we smell of fish.

Angela Kirby

The Poets

Ann Alexander lives in the far South West – as far as you can go without falling into the sea. In her dark past, she was an advertising copywriter in London, and still finds inspiration in the media. She has won several prizes, including first prize in Mslexia 2007, The Frogmore Prize 2000 and Bedford Open 2007, third prize in BBC's Poem for Britain 2003 and recently fourth prize in this year's Peterloo poetry competition. Her two collections from Peterloo are *Facing Demons* and *Nasty, British & Short*.

Alice Beer was born and educated in Vienna but has lived in England since 1939. She surprised herself by starting to write poems in her late seventies, urged by her overwhelming impressions when visiting battlefields in France. She has continued writing ever since, feeling age is no barrier. Her poems have been published by several magazines: *Smiths Knoll*, *The Rialto*, *Envoi* and *Time Haiku*, and in several anthologies, most recently *Images of Women*, Arrowhead 2006. She has published two collections: *Facing Forward, Looking Back*, Poetry Monthly Press 1999 and *Talking of Pots, People and Points of View*, poetry p f 2005

Carole Bromley is married with four children and four grandchildren. She lives in York where she teaches creative writing for the University's Centre for Lifelong Learning. Her poems have been widely published in magazines and anthologies, most recently in *I am twenty people* (ed Mimi Khalvati and Stephen Knight 2007) and *Images of Women* (Myra Schneider and Dilys Wood eds2006). In 2005 her pamphlet collection *Unscheduled Halt* was a winner in the Poetry Business competition and in the same year she won the Bridport Prize for Poetry and read at the Aldeburgh Poetry Festival. She is working on a first full length collection.

Barbara Burford is a co-founder of Grey Hen Press. Her poetry and prose can be found on many teaching modules, and she co-edited *Dancing the Tightrope* (The Women's Press 1987). A former research scientist and civil servant she now runs a business consultancy and is Deputy Director of the Centre for Inclusion and Diversity at the University of Bradford. And she's trying to finish a novel.

Marianne Burton lives in Leicestershire and London. She was awarded a year's mentorship by the poetry magazine *Smiths Knoll* in 2006. She won first prize in the *Mslexia* 2006 competition, and was a prize-winner in the Bridport Poetry Competition 2007. Her pamphlet *The Devil's Cut* (Smiths Knoll) was a 2007 Poetry Book Society Choice.

Christine Coleman grew up in Sussex, and now works in Adult Education in Birmingham. Several of her poems have won prizes and been published in magazines including *Mslexia, Acumen, Poetry Life, Envoi, The Frogmore Papers and The New Writer*. Her work features in *'Four Caves of the Heart'*, an anthology of fourteen women poets (Second Light Publications 2004). Her pamphlet collection is *'Single Travellers'*, (Flarestack, 2004). As part of the poetry ensemble *Late Shift*, she has performed at literary festivals, including Edinburgh. She also writes fiction: *'The Dangerous Sports Euthanasia Society'* Transita 2005. www.christinecoleman.net

Pamela Coren was born in Rochdale in 1949, and read English at UEA, going on to higher degrees at King's College, London and Leicester University. She taught medieval and Renaissance literature in the English department at Leicester until retiring from teaching in 2000 to concentrate on writing. She has since had poems in many magazines and won some prizes. Her first collection, *The Blackbird Inspector* was published by Laurel Books in 2005. She lives in Stamford with her husband and a greyhound, plays the lute, paints abstracts, sings Gregorian chant and publishes academic papers on obscure literary matters.

Kathryn Daszkiewicz was born and brought up in the north east of England and studied English at Leeds University. She now lives and works in Lincolnshire. Kathryn did not start writing until her early thirties and since then has been widely published in good poetry magazines. She was awarded a writer's bursary by East Midlands Arts in 2001 and was selected for their 24-8 project. A selection of her work appeared in the 2001 Shoestring Press anthology of *New Writing* that same year. *In the Dangerous Cloakroom*, her first full-length collection, was published by Shoestring Press in October 2006.

Ann Drysdale was born near Manchester, raised in London, married in Birmingham, ran a smallholding and brought up three children on the North York Moors and now lives in South Wales. She was a journalist for many years, writing, among other things, the longest-running by-line column in the Yorkshire Evening Post. She has won a few prizes and published several books, including a memoir, *Three-three, two-two, five six*, described by Raymond Tallis as "a masterpiece" and a quirky guidebook to the City of Newport. Of her four volumes of poetry from Peterloo, the most recent, *Between Dryden and Duffy*, appeared in 2005. A fifth collection, *Quaint and Offensive*, is scheduled for 2009.

Joanna Ezekiel has had over 60 poems published in magazines, anthologies, journals and ezines including *More Poetry, Envoi, iota* and *Reactions 3*. Pamphlets: *A braid of words* with Poetry Monthly Press, 2003 and *Safe Passage* with White Leaf Press, 2007. Joanna has an MA in Creative Writing and Personal Development from Sussex University. She lives in Twickenham.

Kate Foley was born in London. A former midwife, teacher, then Head of Ancient Monuments Laboratory, she now lives in Amsterdam, where she is a member of the magazine Versal's editorial team. She leads poetry workshops in Holland and England and her 4th collection, *The Silver Rembrandt* was published by Shoestring Press in June 2008.

Angela France is a prize-winning poet who has published regularly in many of the leading journals in the UK and abroad. Angela is also an editor of the poetry journal *'iota'* and of the on-line journal *'The Shit Creek Review'*. She runs a regular live poetry event – *'Buzzwords'* – featuring guest poets and open mic. She is studying, part time, for an MA in Creative and Critical Writing at The University of Gloucestershire and is employed by a small charity working with disengaged and challenging young people. A collection of her poetry is forthcoming from Bluechrome Publishing.

Berta Freistadt has written poetry since she was six. Her work is much anthologised and has been published by Virago, Routledge, *Red Pepper, Nashim, Diva,* and others. Her own pamphlet of poetry - *Flood Warning* - was published by Five Leaves, Nottingham in 2004.

Her prose book *Mass Dreams* was the London Region winner of the Undiscovered Authors 2006 Competition. Berta is now a *discovered* author ! As well as being a sometime writer, she teaches Memoir & Poetry at Birkbeck and Mary Ward. Living alone in London with Mr Charlie-Bluebell next to a cemetery she enjoys the quiet neighbours.

Jude Goodwin's poems can be read in journals including *Cider Press Review, Burnside Review, Comstock Review,* and upcoming in CV2. They have won and been placed well in the IBPC: New Poetry Voices competition, were shortlisted in the CBC Radio Literary Awards, and received Honorable Mention in the Jessie Bryce Niles Chapbook Competition. Jude lives in BC, Canada where she freelances as publisher/editor/author and illustrator for various small journals and papers. www.judegoodwin.com

Joy Howard has lived in West Yorkshire for over twenty years which for someone who shuttled about all over the UK till her late 40s says a lot, but she's not quite sure what about. Poetry has always been part of her life, and her work was frequently anthologised during the 1980s, when she was on a roll. After her retirement in 2005, she returned to writing, and co-founded Grey Hen Press. She won her first ever prize in 2007 and is, as they say, 'working on a first collection'. She is an incurable optimist.

Angela Kirby was born in Lancashire now lives in London. Apart from raising five children, she has worked as, amongst other things, a chef and a garden designer, and has written five books on food and gardening. She has a D.Phil in Creative Writing from Sussex University. Her poems are widely published and have won prizes and commendations in several major competitions. Her first collection, *Mr. Irresistible*, was published by Shoestring Press in 2005, and a second collection is due out in 2008. She gives frequent readings in England, Spain and the USA

Thelma Laycock lives in Leeds. Her work has been published in many magazines and anthologies and has been translated into Italian and Hebrew. She has published three collections of poetry, the latest being 'Chameleon Days' (Feather Press, 2007). The time she spent as a volunteer lay worker amongst the Lakota people of South Dakota has been one of the major influences on her work. She is the editor of an annual poetry magazine, *'Gabriel'*, and enjoys giving readings and workshops in the UK and abroad.

Gill Learner began writing poetry in 2001 and discovered the wonderful world of contemporary verse which she is beginning to feel part of, having now been widely published in anthologies and journals. She was thrilled to win the Poetry Society's Hamish Canham Prize 2008. Brummie by birth, she now lives in Reading and loves its Poets' Café where she was guest poet in May 2007. She is told she buys too many books. In summer she grows ricin – a wonderfully dramatic plant – which makes her husband nervous. For more information, see www.poetrypf.co.uk/gilllearnerpage .

Char March is a multi-award-winning poet and playwright. Her credits include three collections of poetry, six BBC Radio 4 plays and seven stage plays. Her poetry and short fiction have been published widely in magazines and anthologies. She grew up in Central Scotland and now divides her time between the NW Highlands and the Yorkshire Pennines. Four chapters of her first novel have already been published, one of which was runner-up in the prestigious NWP Fiction Award. Char is an experienced tutor in creative writing and performance skills and has worked for organisations all over Britain. She is currently Writer-in-Residence for Leeds Hospitals Trust.

Gerda Mayer was born in Karlsbad, Czechoslovakia, and came to England in 1939 at the age of eleven. Among her collections are a shared one with Florence Elon and Daniel Halpern, *Treble Poets 2* and her *Knockabout Show*, both from Chatto and Windus; *Monkey on the Analyst's Couch*, Ceolfrith Press (a Poetry Book Society Recommendation); *The Candyfloss Tree* (co-authors Norman Nicholson and Frank Flynn), Oxford UP; and *A Heartache of Grass*, Peterloo Poets. Her latest poetry collection is *Bernini's Cat*, Iron Press, 1999. *Prague Winter* (autobiographical prose vignettes) was published by Hearing Eye in 2005.

Gill McEvoy runs three regular poetry events in Chester: Zest! an Open Floor poetry night; the Golden Pear poetry reading group, and The Poem Shed, a workshop group. Gill's work is widely published: *Agenda, The Shop, Smiths Knoll, Other Poetry, Acumen, Envoi, Dream*

Catcher and many others. She had a very nasty run-in with ovarian cancer in 2000 and still has to pinch herself everyday to make sure she's still here (and is always utterly delighted to find she still is!).

Rosemary McLeish was born in 1945 in Glasgow and moved to Yorkshire in 1949. She attended schools in Bradford and Ilkley and studied French, English and Psychology in London. She started writing and painting shortly before moving back to Glasgow, where she still lives, in 1985. Poetry came to her at first on her bicycle, and went back to sleep when she developed M.E. in 1987. After her oldest brother died in 1997 it woke up with a vengeance. Her poems have been published in various magazines and places including Thailand. A first collection is in preparation.

Jenny Morris writes poems and fiction. She has taught in this country and abroad. Her writing has won awards and appeared in many magazines and anthologies. Her latest poetry collection is 'Lunatic Moon' (Gatehouse Press). She lives in Norfolk.

Hilary Murray grew up in Kent but has lived in Yorkshire for over thirty years, and has performed her work at various arts festivals in the region. She is a member of Second Light Network, and a founder member of the Leeds poets' group Borderstones. Her poems have been published in *Gabriel* and *Tadeeb International,* and in the pamphlet *Second Bite* (Grey Hen Press 2007) together with Joy Howard and Gina Shaw, with whom she also gives poetry readings. She regularly tries out her poems at the monthly Wicked Words night in Leeds.

Ruth O'Callaghan is a Hawthornden Fellow, competition adjudicator, interviewer and reviewer. A winner in international poetry competitions, she hosts three poetry venues in London and has both compèred and read at poetry festivals in the U.K. and abroad. Her work is published in many anthologies and magazines, has been translated into Italian, Romanian and German. Her collection *Where Acid Has Etched* is currently being re-printed and her new collection from Bluechrome *A Lope of Time* is due out in Autumn 2008.

Meg Peacocke began to publish poems only in her fifties, though she had written for many years before that. She has four colections from Peterloo Poets, has won several major prizes and was given a Cholmondeley Award in 2005. She is a frrelance tutor and a mentor for The Literary Consultancy.

Judith Priestman was born in 1951 and grew up in rural Oxfordshire, where she still lives and writes poetry about landscape and loss.

Ruth Sharman lives in Bath with her young son and works as a freelance French translator. She has won prizes in the Arvon, National and Cheltenham Festival Poetry Competitions and her poems have appeared in various poetry magazines and national newspapers, and in a number of anthologies including *The Faber Book of Murder, Making Worlds: One Hundred Contemporary Women Poets* and the Staple First Editions series. Her first collection, *Birth of the Owl Butterflies*, was published by Picador.

Clare Shaw grew up in Burnley, spent ten years in Liverpool and now lives in Todmorden. Her first poetry collection, *Straight Ahead* was published by Bloodaxe in 2006. Clare is a popular and engaging performer of her own work, has been published in journals and anthologies, including *Out Of Fashion* and *Answering Back* by Faber and Faber, and has received critical acclaim and awards for her poetry including a "Highly Commended" in the Forward Prize 2006. She is also widely known for her work and publications around women's mental health, and is co-director in a self-harm training partnership: www.harm-ed.co.uk

Gina Shaw lives near Ilkley and started writing in middle age. She has had poems published in *Aireings; The Countryman; First Time; Salvo* and *Smiths Knoll.* She appears together with Joy Howard and Hilary Murray in the pamphlet *Second Bite* , Grey Hen Press 2007

Ruth Silcock was born in Manchester in 1929, read English at Girton College and later became a social worker. She lives in Oxfordshire, and has published several children's books. Three collections of her poetry have been published by Anvil Press: *Mrs Carmichael, A Wonderful View of the Sea* and *Biographies etc.* A successful radio play, *46 Nursing Homes*, was based on a sequence of poems.

Anne Stewart 'discovered' a passion for poetry in her 40s and, five years on, began making a life where poetry was key and where she could make her own serious contribution to the poetry pool. She founded and is editor of *poetry p f*, an on online showcase for poets, and provides freelance technical services to poets and poetry organisations. She has an MA in Creative Writing from Sheffield Hallam University, and is one of the 'Ten Hallam Poets' (Mews Press 2005). Her work has been published in a growing list of magazines and anthologies, including web and e-zines.

Diane Tang was born in the US and moved to London in the '70s. She worked as an editor and copy writer for many years, left work in 2005 for an interesting variety of reasons, and has always somehow managed to fit in poetry wherever it would. She lives in north-west London with husband, and has two grown children and a grandson. Her poems have appeared in a variety of magazines and have won some prizes.

Isobel Thrilling was born in Suffolk, brought up in a mining village in the North East at read English at Hull University. She spent many years as Head of Service for teaching ESOL in a London borough. Her poems have been widely published in magazines and newspapers including The Observer and The New Statesman, and in many anthologies from major publishers. Her work has been broadcast on BBC Television, ITV and BBC Radio 3 and 4. She has won many prizes (including Bridport, Stroud and York) and her fourth collection *The Language Creatures*, was published by Shearsman in 2007.

Christine Webb has worked in education all her life, and has been writing as long as she can remember. *After Babel* was published by Peterloo Poets in 2004, and last year her poem 'Seven Weeks' won the *Poetry London* competition, while 'Salt' won second prize in *Mslexia*. Currently studying with Jo Shapcott and Andrew Motion for a Creative Writing MA, she's working on her next collection, much of which celebrates her partner of 40 years, who died in 2006. She is an intermittent gardener, disorganized cook and occasional traveller, but is tireless in her criticism of our political scene.

Acknowledgments

ANN ALEXANDER: 'The Obituary' *Facing Demons*, Peterloo 2002; 'Bog Lady', Stepmother's Tale', 'A cold café, the three of us,' 'Clean Break' and 'Beware of the Dog' *Nasty, British and Short*, Peterloo 2007. ALICE BEER: 'Intruder' and 'Baker Street Station', *Talking of Pots, People and Points of View*, poetry p f 2005. CAROLE BROMLEY: 'Sisters' published in *Smiths Knoll;* 'Lunch Date' published in *Seam*. HELEN BURKE: 'Message' *The Book of Beyond*, H Burke 2003. BARBARA BURFORD: 'The Nth Day of Christmas' and 'Sisterwrite' *A Dangerous Knowing*, Sheba 1984. MARIANNE BURTON: 'Holy Innocents' published in *Mslexia;* 'Miss You Nights' published in *Anon;* 'The Roses' *The Devil's Cut*, Smiths Knoll 2007. CHRISTINE COLEMAN: 'Goldilocks' published in *Mslexia;* Single Travellers, *Flarestack* 2004; Four Caves of the Heart, *Second Light Publications* 2004. PAMELA COREN: 'Not Suffering the Midnight Owl' and 'The Death's Head Galliard' *The Blackbird Inspector*, Laurel Books 2005. KATHRYN DASZKIEWICZ: 'Black Sheep' published in *Staple;* 'Last Word' published in *Dreamcatcher*. Both poems and 'Revenge Tragedy' *In the Dangerous Cloakroom*, Shoestring Press 2006. ANN DRYSDALE: 'New Fruit': Second Prizewinner in the National Poetry Competition 2001, *Backwork*, Peterloo 2002. JOANNA EZEKIEL: 'The Mermaids of Atlantis Speak' *Safe Passage*, White Leaf Press 2007, 'The Long Journey' published in *Envoi* and *Safe Passage*, White Leaf Press, 2007. KATE FOLEY: 'Goddesses' published in *Sofia*. ANGELA FRANCE: 'Landed' published in *iota;* "A Taste of Ginger published in '*The Shit Creek Review*' (ezine); 'View from the Crossroads' published on website '*Hags, Harlots and Heroines'*. ANGELA KIRBY: 'Misreading the Entrails' and 'The Reunion' published in *Succour;* 'An Aftertaste of Salt' *Mr Irresistible*, Shoestring Press 2005. THELMA LAYCOCK: 'The Cutter's Daughter' was commended in Poetry on the Lake competition 2005. GILL LEARNER: 'Witch' published in *Poetry News* ; 'Ties' published in *Obsessed With Pipework*. GILL MCEVOY: 'Witchcraft' published in *The Journal;* 'Let's Get This Straight' published as 'A Message to the Unwary' in *The Ugly Tree* and '*Uncertain Days'*, Happenstance Press 2006. ROSEMARY McLEISH : 'Here's Another Poem' published in *Acumen*. GERDA MAYER: 'Telephone Call' published in *Ambit* and in *Treble Poets 2* Chatto & Windus 1975. JENNY MORRIS: 'Accident of Birth' and 'Scarlet Woman' *The Sin Eater*, NPF Publications 1993; 'Donna La Morte' (under the title 'Visitation') *Lunatic Moon*, Gatehouse Press 2006. RUTH O'CALLAGHAN: 'Regarding Delivery' published in *Acumen;* 'Marriage' *Not for the Academy*, Onlywomen Press 1999. M R PEACOCKE: 'Revenant' and 'Persephone' *Speaking of the Dead*, Peterloo 2003. 'Wordnurse' and 'No One' *In Praise of Aunts*, Peterloo 2008. J A PRIESTMAN: 'Separating the Sheep from the Goats' Second Prizewinner single poem category in *The New Writer* 2004. RUTH SHARMAN: 'Waterlilies', 'Cobaea Scandens', 'The Dress' and 'The White Garden *Birth of the Owl Butterflies* Picador 1997, 'Metamorphosis' *The Ring of Words*:Poems form the Daily Telegraph Arvon International Poetry Competition 1998. RUTH SILCOCK: 'When I was Twelve', 'The Perils of Ageing', 'The Haunted House' and 'Two Nannies' *Biographies etc,* Anvil Press 2006. ANNE STEWART: 'To Those Who Love Me' *Ten Hallam Poets*, Mews Press 2005; 'This Christmas the Spirit is Rum' 12 Poems, *Twelve Poets Christmas Card set*, poetrypf.co.uk. DIANE TANG: 'Enter Sprite on a Rainy Night' published in *Poetry Nottingham* and *Herga Poets Anthology* 1996. CHRISTINE WEBB: 'Martha' *After Babel*, Peterloo Poets 2004.

Index of Poets

Joy Howard is a co-founder of Grey Hen Press, whose aim is to publish the work of older women. Her poems have featured in several anthologies: *Beautiful Barbarians* (Onlywomen1987), *Dancing the Tightrope* (Women's Press 1987), *Naming the Waves* (Virago 1988), *Not for the Academy* (Onlywomen 1999) and *The Argent Moon* (Pembrokeshire Press 2007). She is a contributor to Grey Hen's first publication *Second Bite*. This is also the name of a group of three older women poets, of which Joy is a founder member, who give readings together. After a long career in social services, she is now re-focusing her energy on poetry, a life-long preoccupation. Shortlisted in several recent competitions, she was a Chapter One Open Poetry prizewinner in 2007. Her poems can be found online at *Guardian Unlimited*, and *poetry p f* and feature in 'Poems While You Wait' at St James's Hospital in Leeds. A publication in *Sofia* is forthcoming.

www.greyhenpress.com